DESIGN DREAMS

VIRTUAL INTERIOR and ARCHITECTURAL ENVIRONMENTS

curated by
MAISON de SABLE

CHRONICLE CHROMA

CONTENTS

INTRODUCTION

by GLORIA FOWLER

This striking visual compendium highlights the work of designers and 3D render artists around the globe who visualize architectural, landscape, and interior designs set in utopian environments. The popularity of these compelling images has become a recent phenomenon on social media platforms such as Instagram. Followers are inspired by these spaces while not always realizing whether they exist in the real world or solely in the Metaverse.

Maison de Sable, French for House of Sand, is London-based designer Charlotte Taylor's studio and popular Instagram account of the same name, which showcases her own designs, and those of her collaborators, as well as the work of others in this genre. For this exhibition-in-a-book, Taylor has curated a selection of projects by many of the leading artists working in CGI today, chronicling the ephemeral, fleeting images that otherwise may eventually vanish. As Taylor points out, being able "to take works that are created and shown almost exclusively in a digital format and immortalize them in print is something quite special. Even more so that my personal practice is very analog and paper oriented, so it is almost a 360-degree return—bringing the projects back to paper and print."

However, this digital genre predominantly ex[ists] on Instagram, where many of the most prolific [de]signer's and artist's images are being repos[ted] onto design-centric feeds and appearing on [mil]lions of screens worldwide. These accounts ha[ve] also created a loose-knit, global community of render artists that follow each other and sometim[es] collaborate on projects from afar while living in s[ep]arate countries around the world. Software to[ols] and 3D modeling programs such as Rhinoceros and rendering engines such as OctaneRender a[nd] Unreal are increasingly available, providing a [uni]versal design language that transcends geograp[hic] boundaries.

Some of the projects featured here are single sta[nd]alone images, while others are more thoroug[hly] designed, complete works that appear ready to [be] built. Taylor's highly stylized collaborations with v[ari]ous artists such as Joe Mortell, Alba de la Fuente, ZY[W] Studio, Cream Atelier, Évoque Lab, and Hann[ah] Lippert, to name a few, are an impressive disp[lay] that showcase a range of aesthetics. The minimal[ist,] rectilinear forms of Taylor's The Residency in Josh[ua] Tree with Alba de la Fuente, delineate a moder[n]ist home with concrete floors and glass walls t[hat] allow for a visual immersion with the distinctively rendered Southern California desert landscape. This home in particular is a convincing trompe l'oeil, where the photorealistic renderings read as photographs of an actual building taken from the pages of a high-design shelter magazine. In contrast, Taylor and ZYVA Studio's Neo-Chemosphere project—an homage to John Lautner's iconic Chemosphere home in Los Angeles—is sited on a super sci-fi, futuristic landscape that appears to exist on another planet—a design that is clearly an imaginative exploration made convincingly compelling through CGI.

Many of the aforementioned artists and others also have their own individual, distinct projects highlighted here as well. Joe Mortell's lush, green indoor-outdoor spaces for Winchester Riverside and the Biophili Conservatory suggest a hopeful, verdant dream of a future that is not in danger of climate change. Hugo Fournier's Folded Sanctuary feels akin to something out of *Dune*, and yet by depicting the sole human figure to be found in the book, it also evokes a connection with the viewer that feels both simultaneously tangible and yet clearly otherworldly and dreamlike.

Additionally, other prominent voices in this CGI. community are included here. Ezequiel Pini, whose studio Six N. Five is based in Barcelona, also creates a formally aesthetic range of architectural projects. Many of these are curvilinear and organic such as the Make Room For Us project which is impossibly sited between two rock formations floating over the ocean. Others like The Japanese Garden evoke a perfectly plausible, Zen environment replete with photorealistic human-scaled details such as tatami mats, floor cushions, and slippers. Likewise, Alexis Christodoulou, with studios in Amsterdam and Cape Town, illustrates in Ceramic Meditation a very tangible space that feels like the ultimate hotel lounge and destination. Paul Milinski, whose studio is in Melbourne, Australia, depicts quintessential seaside, fantasy getaways in both The Pier and Table for Two, blurring the boundary between wishful thinking and reality.

Rather than the modernist design principle of form follows function, in these imagined spaces that are inherently image-based, there is an emphasis on desire, beauty, and mood, through the aesthetic manipulations of form, color, setting, and lighting. There is a unifying tendency to elevate the utopian and the not-quite-attainable aspects of the designs which are at once captivating and seductive. In this zone of almost-could-be-real and unreal, both the creators, their fans, and potential would-be clients are not at the mercy of budget constraints and building codes. Interestingly, this creative freedom that has allowed for such compelling visualizations and convincing portfolios is leading to many of these young designers being offered built commissions as well. Taylor, for instance, is currently completing her first architectural project with Studio Andrew Trotter, in the desert in Utah for Paréa Zion, a new landscape hotel. What originally began as a communication tool within the design industry for architects to visualize and convey a design direction to their clients, has now become so much more on a much wider scale.

While most of the projects found within these pages are personal design explorations, there are likewise many that are now commissioned by high-end product and fashion brands. Advertising agencies are increasingly seeking out render artists to create unique marketing campaigns, thus creating a niche of opportunities for many of the most skilled artists working in the industry. In addition to still images, animations have become increasingly popular as well. Simultaneously, the growing interest in creating and selling non-fungible tokens, or NFTs, has provided yet another innovative and financial avenue for these creators. And with continuing technological developments in virtual reality, there are additional possibilities, the limits to which are still unknown. According to Taylor, whereas currently "personal journeys and experiences in these homes aren't yet possible, they are coming very soon with the developing Metaverse"—no doubt providing even more future opportunities for the Design Dreams of these prolific visionaries.

INTERVIEW

by MASSIMO de CONTI
with CHARLOTTE TAYLOR / MAISON de SABLE

TELL US ABOUT YOUR BACKGROUND.

I was born and raised in London to a creative family; my father is a lighting designer and my mother is a lover of interiors and art. I have held a curiosity for architecture and creation from a young age, obsessively building entire towns from Lego and constructing scaffolding towers in the garden while my parents were out. I pursued a degree in fine arts at Chelsea College of Arts. I was creating large-scale illustrations and sculptures, for which three-dimensional modeling became a great design tool for studying measurements and proportions.

WHAT DOES YOUR OWN DESIGN WORK MEAN TO YOU? AND WHAT IS YOUR ULTIMATE GOAL PROFESSIONALLY?

It is a form of play and an obsession that has captured me since I was a child. Design is my personal expression, my way of understanding architecture. I create homes and spaces that bridge the dreamlike with the tangible, bringing access to these luxury homes even if they don't exist in the physical realm. My goal and my journey is to build physical buildings, and my 3D work is part of this process that allows me to develop ideas.

DO YOU DESIGN PROGRAMMATIC REQUIREMENTS AND A HYPOTHETICAL CLIENT FOR THE PROJECTS? AND HOW DO YOU DETERMINE THE LOCATION AND THE SITE OF EACH OF THE IMAGINARY BUILDINGS?

A lot of the projects are actually initiated by a location. It will be a site/landscape I have come across and been in awe of that often sparks the intention to design a house for that setting. Sometimes we imagine a fictive client in which the different rooms and furniture are tailored for that person and their life.

WHAT IS THE MAIN THING YOU FOCUS ON IN THE ATMOSPHERES YOU CREATE THROUGH THE RENDERINGS? WHAT DO YOU STRIVE FOR WHEN YOU DESIGN AN INTERIOR?

Light is very important and completely frames a space for me. Poetic details in architecture is something that is most intriguing, finding these little corners, perspectives, and movements that are a bit out of the ordinary is what a lot of my research is driven by. I strive to create a balanced space that is almost chaotic in its variant materials and forms but that still has a calmness and common thread through the elements.

WHAT REACTION DO YOU HOPE FOR FROM PEOPLE WHO SEE YOUR WORK?

I hope that the spaces are not too far-fetched so people can still have a relationship with them, and that they are viewed as aspirational places they would love to visit, somewhere in between the tangible and unobtainable.

THE MAIN AIM OF ARCHITECTURE IS CREATING SOMETHING PHYSICAL, TANGIBLE. HOW DO YOU RECONCILE CREATING DIGITAL ARCHITECTURE VERSUS BUILT ENVIRONMENTS?

The digital realm has become its own artform in and of itself, and that has been rewarding creatively. It also is a way to explore designs and test out ideas that can be built. The technology has enabled us to realize these design dreams to a certain extent, and that will likely lead to realizing more built projects. I'm personally really interested in domestic projects and small-scale architecture.

WHO OR WHAT INSPIRES YOU MOST IN TERMS OF DESIGN AND ARCHITECTURE?

Space is my main source of inspiration, predominantly from visiting architecture and through viewing its depiction through books and magazines. I am also very curious about architectural photography; I find great interest in other peoples' works to see how they experience and capture the space. Among my favorite architects of the past are Carlo Scarpa, Lina Bo Bardi, Luis Barragán, Pierre Chareau, and Richard England. Among more contemporary architects, I admire Ricardo Bofill and John Pawson in particular, whose work I love even though it is very minimalistic compared to mine.

DO YOU HAVE A FAVORITE ARCHITECTURALLY DESIGNED RESIDENCE OF ALL TIME?

Out of the ones I've been able to visit in person, I would say, it's between Maison de Verre in Paris by Pierre Chareau or the Sheats–Goldstein Residence in Los Angeles by John Lautner.

HOW DID YOU GO ABOUT CURATING THE LIST OF ARTISTS FEATURED IN THIS BOOK? WHAT WAS THE CRITERIA IN CHOOSING THEM?

The majority of the artists in the book are ones I have worked with in the past years and have built a personal relationship with. Others are prominent designers and 3D artists currently working in this genre and whose work I admire. All of the work shown here represents a high level of design in interiors and architecture, and also showcases the personal style and interests of each creator.

THESE DIGITALLY REALIZED HOMES SEEM TO BE AN IDEAL WORLD ON STEROIDS, LOCATED IN REMARKABLE SETTINGS, WITH THE FINEST SELECTION OF MATERIALS AND FURNITURE. THEY ALSO ALL SEEM TO SHARE A BEAUTIFULLY STERILE AESTHETIC WITH A NOTABLE HUMAN ABSENCE. IS THIS INTENTIONAL?

It is completely intentional that people are absent from the images. I want to leave enough details and similarities that someone can relate to the space and feel an attachment, yet for it to be entirely personal and open to how they would envisage themselves in the space. The human presence is only hinted at with elements like a book or maybe a cigarette, left behind in an otherwise pristine setting.

WHAT ARE THE LIMITATIONS WITHIN THE DIGITAL REALM OF THESE HOMES? HOW WILL TECHNOLOGY AFFECT THIS EXPERIENCE MOVING FORWARD?

Most of these projects are only experienced via static images or animation which is heavily directed by the creator/artist. Personal journeys and experiences in these homes aren't yet possible but are coming very soon with the developing Metaverse. I think that the next step will be the VR experience of the space.

CAN YOU SHARE MORE DETAILS OF FUTURE PROJECTS IN THE METAVERSE?

I am currently working on a few projects for it. The Metaverse world is not stable; it is still a niche community and an area in development that will become more accessible to a wider audience. We are bringing another level of immersive experience to some of the homes and designs beyond their current digital portfolio. It's a really interesting moment where it is becoming possible to bring actual movement and interaction that incorporates the other senses into the experience of these digital homes, and bridging the physical and 3D worlds.

CASA ATIBAIA

Charlotte Taylor / Nicholas Préaud

Located on the Atibaia river in São Paulo, Casa Atibaia is a home that inhabits the forest by coexisting around and in between the landscape rather than imposing on nature. For us, Brazilian modernism is all about living inside with the illusion of being outside, the purity and elegance of ramps and staircases gently swirling around in a contemplative nature with a lightness of glass façades. Casa Atibaia sits between this delicate and airy essence and a more brutal and primitive aspect.

The structure of the home follows the geometric modernist principles yet opens up onto an expansive organic inner courtyard that curves and responds to the surrounding vegetation, bridging a gap between the outside and inside. This boundary is further broken down by the landscape itself acting as a supporting element of the home; the entire structure is built around preexisting rocks as natural pilotis, a more brutalist take on the modernist language. These rocks also occupy the interior to a functional extent; the bathroom and dressing room are carved entirely out of such forms with the smaller rocks acting as furnishing elements, dictating the fluid layout of the home.

The residing furniture is a balance of modernist gems, antique pieces, and more contemporary additions with the likes of Pierre Augustin Rose, Charlotte Perriand, and Pierre Chapo.

THE RESIDENCY IN JOSHUA TREE

Charlotte Taylor / Alba de la Fuente

Joshua Tree residence is inspired by its surroundings. The design is based on a focus on balance; the house allows the interior and exterior to merge. This atmosphere is achieved through sensitive architectural gestures; the colors and textures of the landscape are reflected in the materiality of the house.

 The materiality of the interiors is characterized by a mimicry with the exterior landscape, elements in shades of wood and green. Materials such as concrete, glass, and steel stand out. These materials reflect the landscape and pay attention to how you will feel when you are inside each space.

HELIOPHILIA
Alba de la Fuente

What would it be like to stay living in the last ray of sunset?

Heliophilia is a collection of ten art installations that presents a balance between architecture and digital art. The project delves into the sunset process to identify its elements and concepts, to experiment with them and then transfer them to architecture.

Influenced by natural environments, it explores the architecture focusing on the way of understanding light and shapes. A continuity is created between the environment and the house, through the use of materials and shapes, which allows the expression of sunlight.

Sunlight is the main concept of the project; it is reinterpreted in different ways, highlighting the essence of each space. The installations reflect the representation of these concepts in an architectural context, a house set in a natural coastal environment, reproducing the sunset process in each room in a different way.

Light, materials, and the different elements that compose the space play an essential role to make each installation. The balance between materials, textures, and shapes allows the maximum expression of light. The result is spaces that reflect simplicity and serenity. And it is in this harmony between light and space where captivating plays of light that recall the sunset process are created.

VILLA ORTIZET

Charlotte Taylor / ZYVA Studio

Located in the township of Saint-Pierre-le-Vieux in Lozère, the Villa Ortizet is a tribute to Anthony Authié's grandfather, whom has spent half of his life in this charming and mysterious French village. For this project, Authié drew inspiration from his childhood memories to recall the legends and landscapes

With an area of 260 square meters, the structure of the house is a green monochrome shell as if to mimic the surrounding nature. Balancing between modernist and organic architecture, the design of the space is characterized by a recurrent recourse to the curve and a limited selection of furnitures.

The apparent rock, the common thread linking the different areas, aggregates with the building to form a single entity. By exteriorizing interiorities, this project halfway between life space and spiritual place delivers a contemporary commentary on housing as a management of biological diversity.

By considering nature as a structuring emergence of architecture, Anthony Authié and Charlotte Taylor emancipate themselves from traditional forms of gardens and greenhouses to create a true symbiosis between the built space and the surrounding nature. This hybrid format presents a new type of evolutionary architecture in permanent interaction with the environment and the climate: a sensorial architecture that can be explored through sound, smell, and touch, favoring experience through the interaction of the various elements that compose it.

Rejecting every kind of gadget linked to the green-market, the two designers seek in this project to recreate a link between the user and nature through spatial exploration. By addressing environmental concerns, no longer from a pragmatic standpoint but from architectural and aesthetic experimentations, Charlotte Taylor and Anthony Authié approach the problematic of the contemporary world from a new angle, stimulating the senses and the people's imagination.

NEO-CHEMOSPHERE

Charlotte Taylor / ZYVA Studio

Anthony Authié, founder of ZYVA studio, and Charlotte Taylor, founder of Maison de Sable, present their second collaboration, Neo-Chemosphere, a dreamlike project homage to John Lautner, who designed in 1960 a crazy alien spaceship house in Los Angeles.

In reaction to the covid-19 crisis and climate change, the two designers envisioned a post-anthropocentric existence where their house is staged in a pink world of a fantasized extraterrestrial's archaeological site, somewhere on Massif des Calanques beside the sea.

Within an area of 145 square miles, the structure of the house is an octagon of 14 meters in diameter placed on a concrete pillar stuck between the rocks. The interior is entirly draped with a white resin to create a strong contrast with the pink environment.

Authié and Taylor genuinely created a peaceful and quiet atmosphère in order to make the visitor feel calm and relaxed, in a contemplative state of mind, ready to meet with the beauty of the surrounding outside world.

Exteriorizing interiorities, this project halfway between life space and spiritual place delivers a contemporary commentary on housing as retirement from society and reconnection with nature. The two designers seek to create a metaphysical relationship between architecture and its user.

Balancing between modernist and sci-fi, the design space is also a tribute to the cinematographic visuals effects that emerged in the mid-'70s.

Alien, *2001: a Space Odyssey*, *Star Wars*, and *Rollerball* are among the main inspirations. These iconic films were the first forms of an exaggerated future removing us from an insipid reality.

Like a romantic odyssey, this place bring us back to basics, the beauty of loneliness, the aesthetics of a nature that offers unsuspected colors, and the possibility of considering new worlds beyond the seas.

VILLA SARACENI

Charlotte Taylor / Riccardo Fornoni / Cream Atelier

Villa Saraceni is a place where humans and nature could share the pleasure of living, where the artifice and the landscape could join organically. Situated nestled into the white cliffs of Scala dei Turchi, a landscape with a wealth of natural sculptural forms, the design of house takes inspiration from its surroundings with the architecture almost growing from the rock formations.

VILLA SARACENI Charlotte Taylor / Riccardo Fornoni / Cream Atelier / 65

VILLA VENEZIA
Charlotte Taylor / Évoque Lab

The intention behind the Villa Venezia project was to pay homage to the remarkable Carlo Scarpa's body of work, reinterpreting his language and some of the main themes, designing a dream villa in continuous connection with water. The large spaces and the overlapping of horizontal and vertical planes are the main themes of the project, which give the entire space depth and visual richness, all linked by the pervasive presence of water visible in multiple forms, such as pools and through the caustics that are reflected on the different surfaces. The selection of materials was made by drawing on the repertoire of Scarpa's architecture and Venetian culture. The spaces are populated by a selection of furnishings from the work of Carlo and Tobia Scarpa and some pieces made in the same historical period, with some exceptions.

THE JAPANESE GARDEN

Six N. Five / Ezequiel Pini / Joan García Pons /
Simon Kaempfer

The Japanese Garden series combines classical elements of
Japanese architecture with stylized flora to create scenes that
perfectly capture the culture's desire for simplicity. Portraying
the minimal, surreal, and tranquil atmosphere of Japan, we
tried to carry a consistent design language throughout each
image using elements such as perfectly pruned trees, birch
wood accents, and overcast mountain landscapes. The result
was these surreal and pleasant compositions surrounded by
green and nature.

ICELAND HOUSE

Charlotte Taylor / Évoque Lab

Iceland House is a project that aims to underline how architecture, design, and digital art can coexist.

The idea was born from a desire to have a residence totally immersed in the natural context of Iceland, the house on stilts in total connection with nature and an ever-changing landscape.

Hence the decision to have a building with a totally glazed perimeter with movable steel walls, allowing a continuous dialogue with nature, transparencies, and reflections. It's a mirror on the river, reflecting the image of the sky, the stream of the river, and the high ridge of the surrounding canyon.

Just like the facade of the building, the interior also subordinates everything to harmony with nature and the unparalleled view.

A few sophisticated and minimal furnishings were selected. The selected objects have a handcrafted style and use materials such as steel and wood. Everything has been rigorously positioned inside the open space, allowing the view of the landscape to manifest itself from any point of the house. Neutral materials were chosen to underline the furnishings.

ORGANIC LOUNGE Hugo Fournier / 105

ARJÉ X NORDIC KNOTS

Nicholas Préaud / Évoque Lab

Nordic Knots is launching a new collection, together with New York City-based lifestyle brand Arjé, that explores the meaning of finding home. While on the surface these two brands embrace different aesthetics, the vibrant history of the Mediterranean on the one hand and the sharp, understated coolness of northern Europe on the other, a friendship between the brands and the similarity of their visions have led to a partnership in which each has found a home with the other. Since rugs play such a vital role in making a bare space feel like a home, the nature of the collaboration feels particularly fitting. In the search for a home for this new collection, Paris-based 3D artist Nicholas Préaud created the Arjé x Nordic Knots Home, a dreamscape world that aims to, just like the rug designs intend to, merge the homes of the two brands. The result is an imagined place that does not, in reality, exist, where the idyllic Swedish archipelago meets the raw and warm earth of southern Spain. In this dream home, the sleek Scandinavian minimalism is present in the architecture and color palette, whilst the rustic richness of the Mediterranean is reflected in the selection of materials, details, and objects. A dreamed-up utopia that is emblematic of the Arjé x Nordic Knots Collection: a new kind of home that is just waiting to be created.

UTAH HOUSE FOR PAREA ZION

Charlotte Taylor / Studio Andrew Trotter /
Klaudia Adamiak

Utah House is the first design by Charlotte Taylor that will come
to life as a concrete building. The project is led by Andrew
Trotter for Paréa Zion, situated in the landscapes of Zion, Utah.
The house bridges inside and outside spaces with kinetic furnishings and movable architectural details as the basis of the
design language.

ÅLAND ISLANDS VILLA

Charlotte Taylor / Odd in Shape

Sparked by 'The Houses of The Future' 1960s series of illustrations by Charles Schridde and various vintage interiors,
we explored the notion of futurism in architecture through a
dated lens. Applying design details from sci-fi films of the era,
'60s Californian home advertising, and artistic visions on the
topic, we developed a number of fictional villas in far-flung
landscapes and locations.

MAKE ROOM FOR US

Six N. Five / Ezequiel Pini / Jesús Mascaraque /
Nil Estany / Thiago Tallman / Andy Lipe / Julia Ippolito /
Artur de Menezes

Humans modify, adapt, and ultimately destroy what mother nature freely offered to us. Home, the Earth, is all we have. It is our plan A and also, plan B.

Make Room for Us is an architectural project in the digital universe, which not only proposes to adapt architecture to nature. It speaks of our repentance and forgiveness for the damage we have caused in the physical world. Now it is our turn to adapt to what has always existed.

Through adaptive designs that mimic cellular organisms, we propose an architectural system that interacts with nature in an imaginary ecosystem of cliffs, mountains, and virtual dreamscapes. This exploration is nothing more than a narrative translated into visual concepts that aim to learn and respond to our environment, to make ourselves our home.

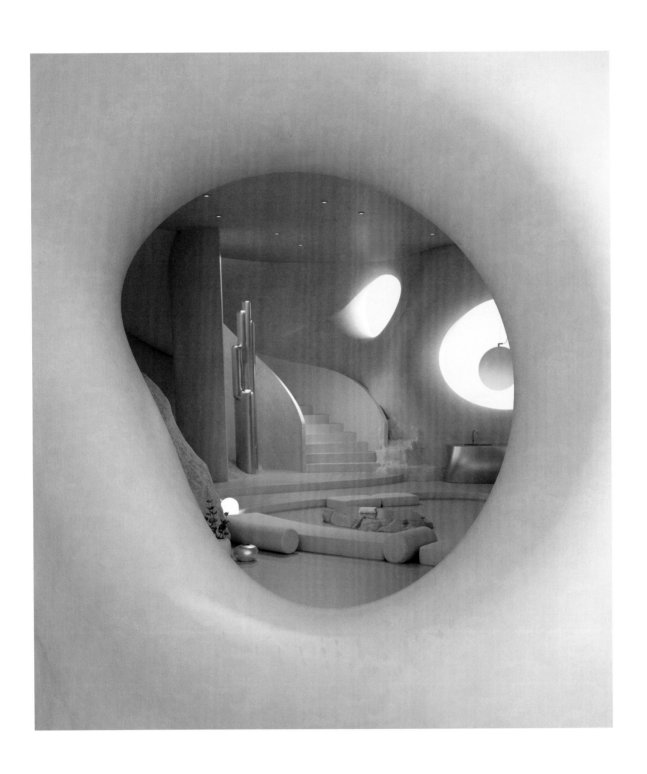

VILLA DEL SOFFIO

Charlotte Taylor / Nicholas Préaud

Villa del Soffio is an experimental home niched in the cliffs of Puglia, Italy. The structure acts as a bridge between both sides of the beach, allowing for a generous double-height space with a minimal footprint in the natural landscape. The house is composed of two slabs glazed on each side, overlooking the raw vertical cliffs to the west and the Adriatic Sea to the east.

The interior layout works as one continuous space with no interruptions and is punctuated by two layers of curtains where privacy is needed: a first layer on the open mezzanine overlooking the living spaces and a second double-height layer all around the house. This project questions the relationship we entertain with our environment by re-imagining the shape and foundation of the house itself.

LIVING COLORS

Six N. Five / Ezequiel Pini

The colorful version of our dream living room. The goal was to create by playing to compose the frame with colors, shapes, and textures, using them in the best way possible. The result is this image that looks like an interior.

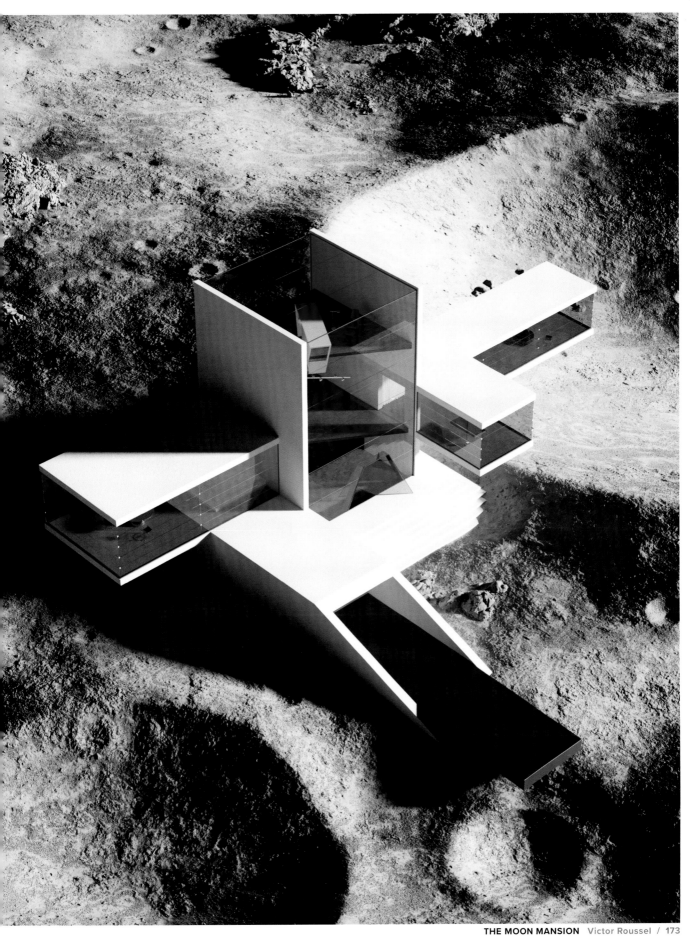

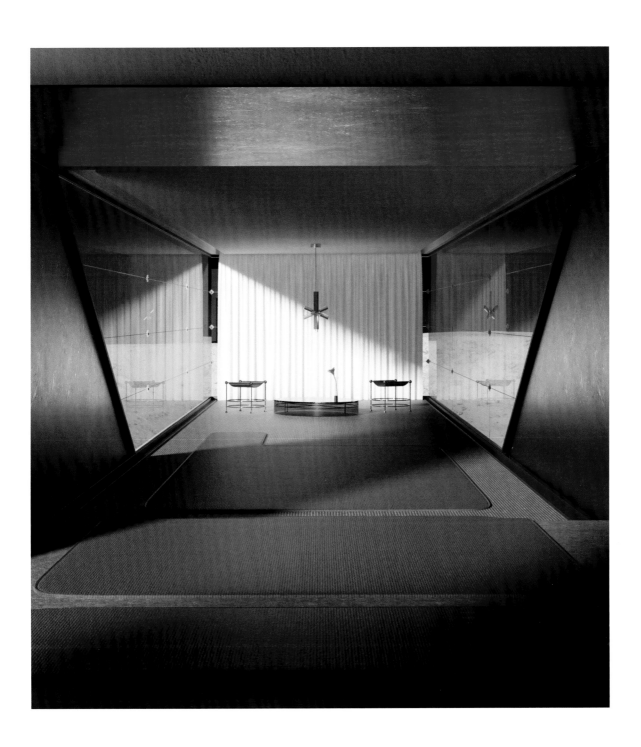

THE ORB

Alba de la Fuente

Challenged to consider questions about the design, functionality, and utility of digital architecture and NFTs, Alba de la Fuente and Tom Dixon came together to attempt a fusion of virtual architecture and lighting design.

The collection of four NFTs consists of an architectural edifice conceived as a lighting object.

Each NFT demonstrates reductive architecture and a dreamlike land and waterscape in different states of luminosity—some from the environment, some from reflections, and some emitting from the structure itself.

In the perpetual search for the purest forms, we have explored the sphere, where The Orb represents a balance between minimalist architecture, materials, and textures, allowing for the maximum expression in digital space of the concept of light objects.

WHAT IF?
ACT ONE: THE JOURNEY

Six N. Five / Ezequiel Pini

Imagination is a uniquely human ability to visualize unlimited possibilities starting with a simple question: What If? Here we raise our voices to wonder about the next steps of humankind and a possible future move. We divided this collection into the following three acts.

Act One explores the perception of time, loneliness, and expectations. It represents the hope to arrive but also the attachments of our mundane life, carrying memories of a previous reality. Finding places and objects of our current everyday life that remind us that we are still not there, while playing with the idea of a new culture, tales, and sagas being told from generation to generation as our ancestors used to do.

WHAT IF?
ACT TWO: "THE SETTLEMENTS"

Six N. Five / Ezequiel Pini

Act Two is a reflection from a far distance that allows us to imagine how life could look in another physical condition. It's probably inaccurate under the eyes of the science community, but it expresses our freedom to dream and to imagine how our homes far away would look like.

WHAT IF?
ACT THREE: "THE ENCOUNTER"

Six N. Five / Ezequiel Pini

A look from inside, the vestiges of our presence in an inhabited and quiet place. They are an involving waltz, represented by objects that encounter each other in different contexts. It is a dance in the silence. Surprise, fear, amazement, and curiosity share the same frame of time.

FEATURED ARTISTS

**ALEXIS CHRISTODOULOU STUDIO /
ALEXIS CHRISTODOULOU**
alexiscstudio.com
@teaaalexis

BUREAU BENJAMIN / BENJAMIN GUEDJ
bureaubenjamin.com
@bureaubenjamin

SARAH CASTAY
@sarah.castay

BENOIT CHALLAND
benoitchalland.com
@benoitchalland

CREAM ATELIER / RICCARDO FORNONI
riccardofornoni.com
@creamatelier
@Riccardo.fornoni

**ÉVOQUE LAB /
EMANUELE LONGO, PAOLA FRASCERRA**
evoquelab.com
@evoquelab

RAFAEL EIFLER
eifler.work
@eifler.work

HUGO FOURNIER
hugofournier.com
@hugo.fournier

FORMUNDRAUSCH / HANNES LIPPERT
formundrausch.de
@formundrausch

ALBA DE LA FUENTE
@albadlfuente_

MAISON DE SABLE / CHARLOTTE TAYLOR
studiocharlottetaylor.com
@maison_de_sable
@charlottetaylr

PAUL MILINSKI
milinski.studio
@paul_milinski

GONZALO MIRANDA
@gonzzzalo.m

JOE MORTELL
@joemortell

**ODD IN SHAPE /
FEDOR KARCUBA, KATIA TOLSTYKH**
oddinshape.com
@oddinshape
@fedor.katcuba
@katia_tolstykh

NOVA VISUALIS
novavisualis.com
@novavisualis

JORIS POGGIOLI
jorispoggioli.com
@jorispoggioli

NICHOLAS PRÉAUD
nicholaspreaud.co
@nicholaspreaud

VICTOR ROUSSEL
victorroussel.com
@vic.rou

SIX N. FIVE / EZEQUIEL PINI
sixnfive.com
@sixnfive
@mascaraque

SPOT STUDIO / NICOLAS CANELAS
spotstudio.es
@spotstudio.es

S T O A / ALIN STOICA
stoa.ro
@stoa.arh

**STUDIO ANDREW TROTTER /
KLAUDIA DAMIAN**
andrew-trotter.com
@studioandrewtrotter

**3DD FACTORY /
DIEGO RAPUZZI, DYLAN CAMPARDO**
3ddfactory.com
@3dd_factory

GEORGE TYEBCHO
@george_tyebcho

KASIA WILK
@wilk_kj
wilk.studio

ZYVA STUDIO
zyvastudio.com
@zyvastudio**

Design Dreams curated by Maison de Sable

Publishers: Gloria Fowler, Steve Crist
Editor and Art Director: Gloria Fowler
Design and Production: Alexandria Martinez
Production: Freesia Blizard
Copy Editor: Sara DeGonia

ISBN: 978-1-7972-2016-1

Library of Congress Cataloging-in-Publication
Data available.

Manufactured in China

CHRONICLE CHROMA

Chronicle Chroma is an imprint of Chronicle Books
Los Angeles, California

Follow us on Instagram @chroniclechroma

chroniclechroma.com